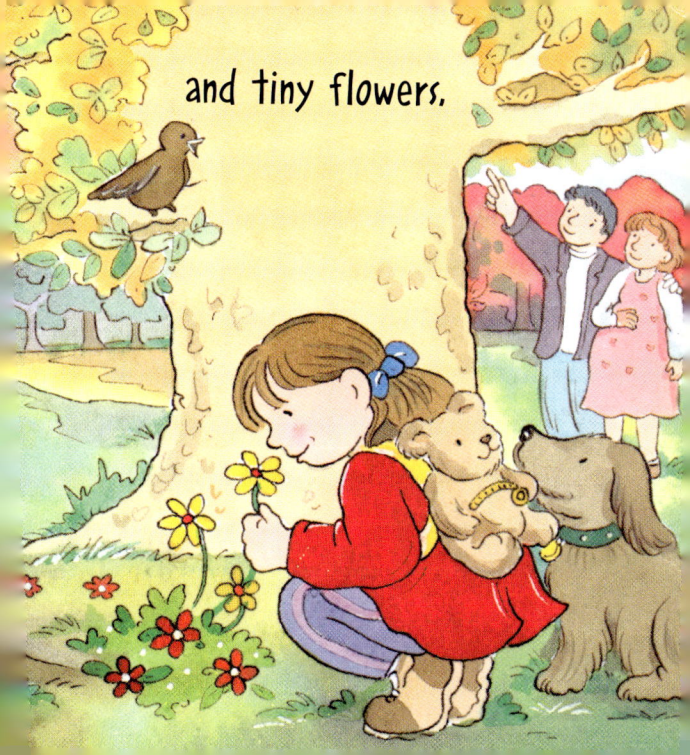

Thank you for making the warm yellow sun

and the blue sea.

Thank you for making all the animals,

big ones and small ones.

Thank you for sending rain to help our food grow.

Thank you for water to drink.

Thank you for
making the rainbow
after the rain.
It's a sign of how much
you love us.